What is climate?

Bobbie Kalman

Crabtree Publishing Company

www.crabtreebooks.com

Big Science Ideas

Created by Bobbie Kalman

*For Steven and Edith Bankovich,
two of the most caring people on Earth.
The whole family is grateful for everything you do.*

**Author and
Editor-in-Chief**
Bobbie Kalman

Editor
Kathy Middleton

Proofreader
Crystal Sikkens

Design
Bobbie Kalman
Katherine Berti
Samantha Crabtree
　(logo and front cover)

Photo research
Bobbie Kalman

Print and production coordinator
Katherine Berti

Prepress technician
Katherine Berti

Photographs
Corel: page 25 (top)
Louie Schoeman / Shutterstock.com: title page
Rufous / Shutterstock.com: page 9
Thor Jorgen Udvang / Shutterstock.com: page 20
All other images by Shutterstock

Library and Archives Canada Cataloguing in Publication

Kalman, Bobbie
　What is climate? / Bobbie Kalman.

(Big science ideas)
Includes index.
Issued also in electronic formats.
ISBN 978-0-7787-2773-6 (bound).--ISBN 978-0-7787-2778-1 (pbk.)

　1. Climatology--Juvenile literature. I. Title.
II. Series: Kalman, Bobbie. Big science ideas

QC981.3.K34 2012　　　j551.6　　　C2011-907687-X

Library of Congress Cataloging-in-Publication Data

Kalman, Bobbie.
　What is climate? / Bobbie Kalman.
　　p. cm. --　(Big science ideas)
　Includes index.
　ISBN 978-0-7787-2773-6 (reinforced library binding : alk. paper) -- ISBN 978-0-7787-2778-1 (pbk. : alk. paper) -- ISBN 978-1-4271-7842-8 (electronic pdf) -- ISBN 978-1-4271-7957-9 (electronic html)
　1. Climatology--Juvenile literature. I. Title.

QC981.3.K35 2012
551.6--dc23

2011046112

Crabtree Publishing Company

www.crabtreebooks.com　　　1-800-387-7650

Printed in Canada/012012/MA20111130

**Published in Canada
Crabtree Publishing**
616 Welland Ave.
St. Catharines, Ontario
L2M 5V6

**Published in the United States
Crabtree Publishing**
PMB 59051
350 Fifth Avenue, 59th Floor
New York, New York 10118

**Published in the United Kingdom
Crabtree Publishing**
Maritime House
Basin Road North, Hove
BN41 1WR

**Published in Australia
Crabtree Publishing**
3 Charles Street
Coburg North
VIC 3058

Contents

Weather and climate

Is it sunny, hot, and dry?
Is it warm enough to go swimming?
Is it cloudy and **humid**? Will it rain?
Has the **temperature** changed
since last night or this morning?
Do I need to wear a jacket?
Is it windy? Is it cold?
Will it snow today?

Weather forecasts

Weather is what it is like outside right
now. It changes from day to day, and
sometimes from minute to minute.
Many people listen to **weather
forecasts** each morning to find out
which clothes they should wear or
whether they will need an umbrella.
Climate is the usual kind of weather
that an area has at certain times of the
year. This usual weather pattern has
been in the area for many years.

4

Weather words

Sunshine, clouds, wind, **precipitation**, **air pressure**, humidity, and temperature are all parts of weather.

• Temperature is a measure of how hot or cold something is.

• Precipitation is rain, snow, or both.

• Humidity is the amount of **water vapor** in the air (see page 7).

• Air is made up of a number of gases. These gases press down hard on Earth's surface, causing a force called air pressure. High, or strong, pressure brings clear, dry weather. Low, or weak, pressure causes wet, windy, and cloudy weather.

*A **hygrometer** shows the humidity in air.*

*A **barometer** measures air pressure.*

*A **thermometer** measures temperature. This thermometer shows temperature in both Fahrenheit and Celsius degrees.*

*An **anemometer** measures how fast the wind is blowing.*

Air and water

All weather takes place in part of the **atmosphere**.
The atmosphere is a wide band of air around
Earth. It is shown on this globe as a light blue
ring around Earth. Water covers
three-quarters of Earth's
surface. The dark blue
areas on this globe of
Earth are oceans.

atmosphere

Arctic Ocean

Atlantic Ocean

Southern Ocean

The five oceans on Earth are the
Pacific Ocean, Atlantic Ocean, Indian
Ocean, Southern Ocean, and Arctic Ocean.
Which two are not shown on this globe?

Cloud layer

The part of the atmosphere where weather takes place is called the **troposphere**. The troposphere is the cloud layer. It stretches from Earth's surface to the area in the sky where clouds form.

The water cycle

The sun's heat warms Earth's surface and the water on it. The water **evaporates** and changes to water vapor. When wind carries water vapor high into the air, the water vapor gets colder. It **condenses**, or changes to liquid water, which forms clouds. The water in the clouds then falls back down as rain or snow.

High in the atmosphere, air cools. Water droplets form in the air. Many water droplets form clouds.

water vapor

Rain or snow falls and becomes part of oceans, lakes, and rivers.

All kinds of storms

Storms are part of the weather in every kind of climate. Most storms cause heavy precipitation. Precipitation falls from clouds to the ground in liquid or solid form. Sometimes precipitation is a mixture of liquid and solid water. **Sleet** is a mixture of ice pellets and rain or snow.

Wild winds

Wind is air in motion. When the sun heats the land, the air above the ground warms up, too, and begins to rise. Cold air, which is heavier than warm air, then rushes underneath. This rushing air is wind. Wind can blow hard enough to destroy buildings and uproot trees. Strong winds can destroy whole towns!

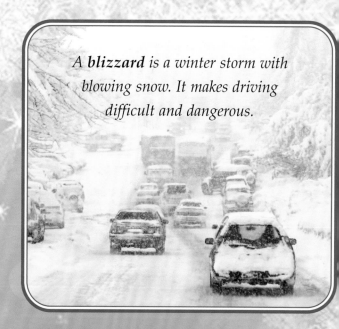

*A **blizzard** is a winter storm with blowing snow. It makes driving difficult and dangerous.*

*Lightning is electricity that builds up in clouds. It creates thunder. **Thunderstorms** often cause heavy rain and strong winds.*

8

Tornadoes are violent storms that begin as **funnel clouds**. Funnel clouds are fast-spinning columns of air.

Hurricanes are large destructive storms with fast-moving winds. They form over warm oceans and drop a lot of rain when they reach land.

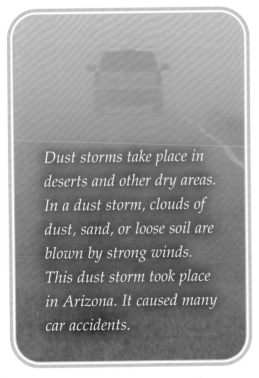

Dust storms take place in deserts and other dry areas. In a dust storm, clouds of dust, sand, or loose soil are blown by strong winds. This dust storm took place in Arizona. It caused many car accidents.

Storms often cause huge floods. People can lose their homes, possessions, and lives in floods.

Looking at Earth

The climate of an area depends on where on Earth that place is located. There are several types of climates. If you look at a globe, you can see that two areas of the world are covered in ice and snow. They are at the top and bottom of Earth. The **North Pole** is the most northern point on Earth. The most southern point on Earth is the **South Pole**. The weather is cold year round near the poles. Both areas have a **polar** climate.

Dividing Earth

The **equator** is an imaginary line across the middle of Earth that divides the planet into two equal parts. The **Northern Hemisphere** is the top half of Earth from the equator to the North Pole. The **Southern Hemisphere** is the bottom half of Earth from the equator to the South Pole.

The hottest places

The weather is hot year round in places near the equator. The warmest temperatures can be found between two other imaginary lines on each side of the equator—the **Tropic of Cancer** and the **Tropic of Capricorn**. The areas between these two lines have a **tropical** climate. Some tropical areas are dry; others get a lot of rain.

NORTH POLE

Arctic

NORTHERN HEMISPHERE

TROPIC OF CANCER

EQUATOR

TROPIC OF CAPRICORN

SOUTHERN HEMISPHERE

Antarctica

SOUTH POLE

Tilted Earth

During the year, Earth moves in one complete circle around the sun. Earth is **tilted**, or not straight up and down. When Earth circles the sun, parts of the planet are tilted toward the sun at different times. This causes the seasons to change. In winter, areas receive less sunlight and heat because they are tilted away from the sun. In summer, temperatures are warmer because areas are tilted closer toward the sun's light and heat.

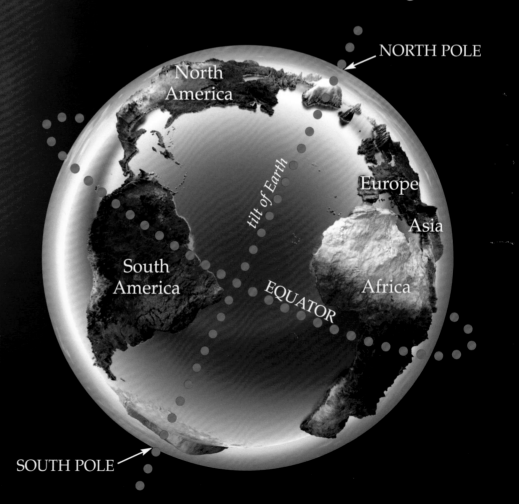

SUN

NORTH POLE

North America

Europe

Asia

South America

Africa

tilt of Earth

EQUATOR

SOUTH POLE

This diagram shows the seasons in the Northern Hemisphere.
It takes Earth 365 days to travel once around the Sun.

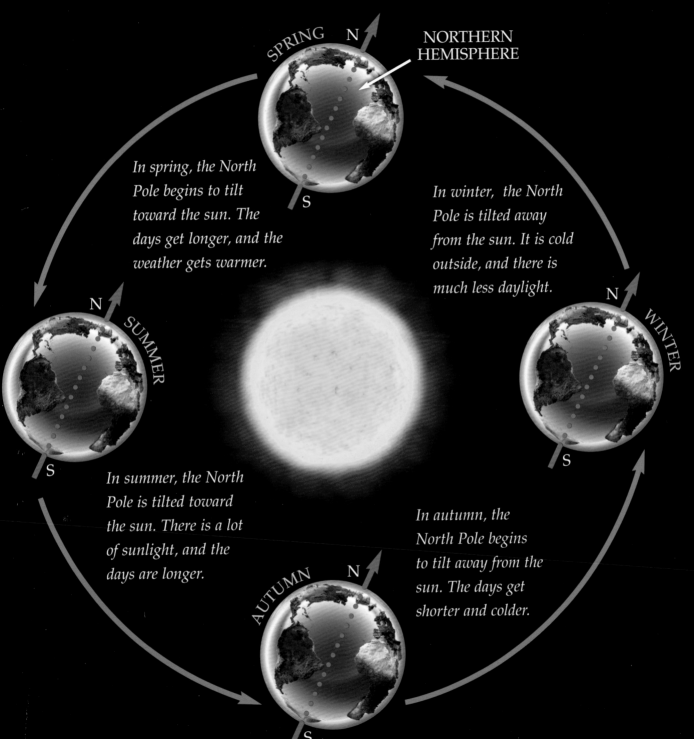

SPRING N

NORTHERN
HEMISPHERE

In spring, the North
Pole begins to tilt
toward the sun. The
days get longer, and the
weather gets warmer.

S

In winter, the North
Pole is tilted away
from the sun. It is cold
outside, and there is
much less daylight.

N

WINTER

N

SUMMER

S

S

In summer, the North
Pole is tilted toward
the sun. There is a lot
of sunlight, and the
days are longer.

In autumn, the
North Pole begins
to tilt away from the
sun. The days get
shorter and colder.

AUTUMN N

S

Four seasons

In both the Northern Hemisphere and Southern Hemisphere, many areas have four seasons each year. The seasons are spring, summer, autumn, and winter. Seasons are part of climate because the weather in each season stays about the same for a long time. The seasons in the Northern Hemisphere are the opposite of the seasons in the Southern Hemisphere at the same times of the year. When it is winter in the north, it is summer in the south.

This part of Earth is tilted away from the sun.

It is a cold and snowy winter day. It is a perfect day for building a snowman!

In spring, this part of Earth starts tilting toward the sun. The weather is warm, and flowers bloom. It is a great time to be outdoors.

Summer days are long, sunny, and hot. This place is tilted toward the sun.

In autumn, this place on Earth begins to tilt away from the sun. The leaves of many kinds of trees turn color and fall off. The weather is colder, so people wear hats and warm sweaters or jackets. Winter will be here soon!

Earth's coldest place

Both the South Pole and North Pole regions are covered by snow and ice all year long. During the winter months, there is no daylight at either pole. During the summer, there are 24 hours of daylight.

Cold Antarctica

The **continent** of Antarctica is at the South Pole. Nearly all of Antarctica is covered by ice. It has the coldest climate on Earth! The climate is called polar. Antarctica has just two seasons— summer, which lasts three months, and nine months of freezing winter. The only people who live in Antarctica are scientists doing research on subjects such as climate, oceans, and animals.

This research team is studying climate. The team was brought to this place by helicopter.

Very few animals

Not many kinds of animals can live on Antarctica, but some penguins, seals, and birds can. Penguins and seals have **blubber**, which is a thick layer of fat under their skin. Blubber keeps heat inside the bodies of animals.

The Weddell seal is a large seal that lives in the Southern Ocean around Antarctica.

Penguin parents feed their chicks by bringing up food for them from their stomachs.

*The South Polar skua is a large bird that **breeds** on Antarctic coasts. It spends its winters in warmer oceans. This bird eats mainly fish. This skua has two small **chicks**, or baby birds.*

North Pole and the Arctic

The north polar region is known as the Arctic. It is made up entirely of the Arctic Ocean, which is mostly covered in frozen ice. Like Antarctica, this region has a polar climate. It is covered by snow and ice all year long, and there is no daylight during the winter months. During the summer, it does not get dark, even at night.

This map shows the Arctic Ocean and the countries around it. Many people live in parts of the Arctic.

Frozen tundra

The **Arctic Circle** includes the lands around the North Pole. It includes parts of Canada, the United States, Norway, Russia, and the island of Greenland. These areas have a **polar tundra** climate.

*The tundra is a huge treeless area covered by **permafrost**, or frozen soil. In summer, the top layer of the soil thaws, but the ground beneath is permanently frozen. Trees cannot grow in this frozen ground, but some plants can. Tundra plants grow low on the ground, where they are sheltered from the strong winds that blow.*

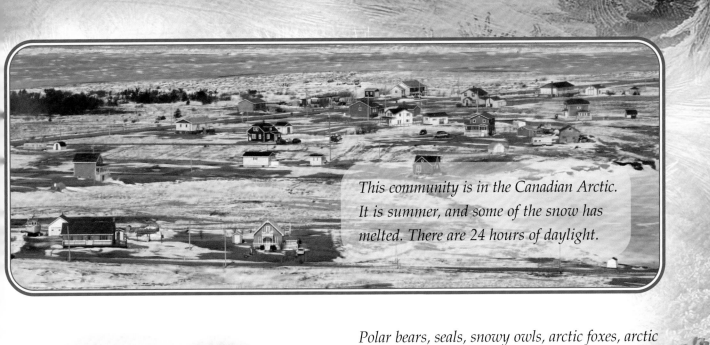

This community is in the Canadian Arctic. It is summer, and some of the snow has melted. There are 24 hours of daylight.

Polar bears, seals, snowy owls, arctic foxes, arctic wolves, and caribou, or reindeer, are a few of the animals that live in the Arctic.

polar bear

snowy owl

Tundra plants are eaten by animals such as deer, arctic hares, sheep, and many kinds of insects.

This arctic animal is a caribou, or reindeer. It feeds on arctic plants.

19

Tropical wet climate

The hottest and wettest part of Earth is at the equator. The climate in this area is called **tropical rainforest** climate. Rain forests have at least 68–78 inches (175–200 cm) of rainfall each year. Tropical rain forests are found in the continents of South America, Asia, Africa, and in the southern parts of North America. A **monsoon** is a strong wind that blows in many tropical areas. It brings heavy rains that last for several months. This period is called the **rainy season**.

During the rainy season, there is much flooding. This flood is in Thailand, a country near the equator. Water covers the roads and has destroyed many homes.

Tropical dry climate

A **tropical savanna** climate is hot. It has a long **dry season** with very little rain. This climate can be found in many areas of the continents of Africa and South America, as well as in the countries of India and Australia. During the dry season, there is less than 2.4 inches (60 mm) of rain. In summer, there are storms with lightning and loud thunder. It rains, and strong winds blow.

This cheetah lives in a savanna in Africa. A savanna is a large, flat grassland that has a few bushes but not many trees. The weather is hot and dry for most of the year.

High on mountains

The climate on tall mountains is not the same as the climate on the lands below. If the mountain is high enough, it will have snow on it, even if it is near the equator. The farther up a mountain you go, the colder the air gets.

*Mount Kilimanjaro is the highest mountain in Africa. Its **peak**, or top, is covered with snow. At its **base**, or bottom, is a savanna. The climate is hot and dry there.*

Tall mountains

The Himalayas stretch across six countries in Asia. The highest peaks on Earth, including Mount Everest, are found there. Near the tops of these mountains, winter lasts from October through to May or June and is both dry and very cold.

Yaks have long hair to keep them warm. They can breathe the thin air high in the Himalayas, which has less oxygen.

This young girl is skiing on the tall Alps in Europe. It is very cold but sunny at the top.

These bighorn sheep live in the Rocky Mountains. The "Rockies" are in western North America.

*High in the Andes Mountains in South America, the climate is called **alpine tundra**, which is like the climate near the Arctic. The same kinds of plants grow in both places.*

Dry deserts

Deserts are areas that get less than ten inches (25 cm) of rain or snow a year. They can be found on every continent, but they are not usually found near the equator. This map shows some of the deserts on Earth. Most of the continent of Antarctica is a desert. It gets less than eight inches (20 cm) of snow in a year. It is the coldest, driest, and windiest desert on Earth.

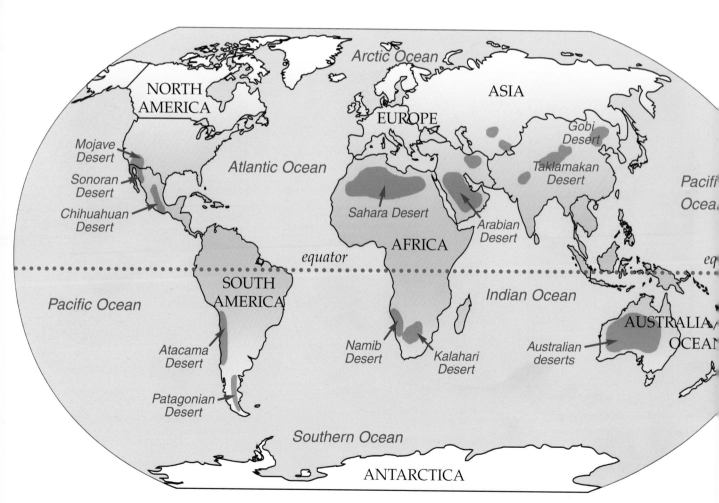

Sand and rocks

Some deserts are hot during the day and cold at night. Some deserts get rain for parts of the year. The Sahara Desert in Africa is the biggest hot desert. Part of it has huge **dunes**, or sand hills. Dunes form when piles of sand are pushed around by strong winds. Few plants grow in sandy deserts like this because there is very little water. Camels, shown below, are among the few animals that can live in sandy deserts. They can go for a week or longer without water, depending on how hot it is.

The Sonoran Desert in North America has two rainy seasons. Many plants and animals live there. These animals are kit foxes.

sand dune

The desert area above, called Monument Valley, is on the border of Utah and Arizona in the United States. It is covered in rocks and is dusty and dry.

Warm ocean currents

Oceans cover three-quarters of Earth. Ocean waters are always moving. Warm and cold **currents** flow through the oceans like rivers. How they move affects the climate, even on land.

The Gulf Stream

The **Gulf Stream** is a warm ocean current that starts at the tip of Florida and follows the eastern coastlines of the United States and Canada before it crosses the Atlantic Ocean. The Gulf Stream warms the climate of the east coast of North America from Florida to Newfoundland and across the ocean to the west coast of Europe.

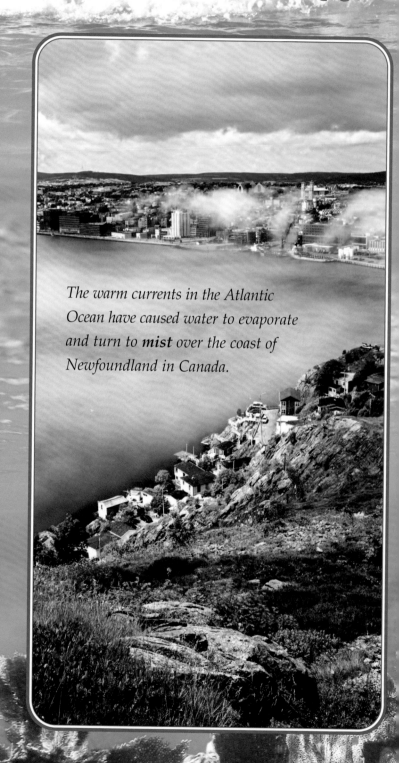

*The warm currents in the Atlantic Ocean have caused water to evaporate and turn to **mist** over the coast of Newfoundland in Canada.*

Milder climates

Areas that are not close to the equator but are close to oceans have **temperate**, or mild climates. Summers are cool and dry, and winters are not very cold. Most of the rain falls during the winter. California, British Columbia, and parts of Europe have mild climates.

This family enjoys the mild climate in California.

Climate change

Climate change is causing ice to melt into the oceans. Animals in the Arctic, such as polar bears and walruses, hunt for food in the ocean and on sea ice. Polar bears hunt seals when they come up for air at breathing holes. They also need the ice to use as a table for eating the seals. Less ice means fewer places in the ocean to eat when polar bears hunt.

Scientists believe that the climate on Earth is changing, and that Earth is warming up. **Climate change** is caused by **greenhouse gases**, such as carbon dioxide. Greenhouse gases are created when we burn oil, natural gas, and coal. They trap the sun's heat in the atmosphere the way glass traps heat in a greenhouse.

Big changes on Earth

Even the smallest temperature changes on Earth can cause big changes in our environment. In some places, climate change causes extreme heat and **droughts**, or long periods with no rain. In other places, climate change causes heavier than usual storms and flooding.

Melting glaciers

Earth is getting warmer, and more ice is melting, and it is melting faster than usual. **Glaciers** are slow-moving rivers of ice. The glaciers at the North Pole and South Pole, as well as on many high mountains, such as the Himalayas and Mount Kilimanjaro, are melting very fast. Glaciers help keep Earth cool because ice reflects the sun's rays. A small amount of the melting ice in glaciers also provides water for many people. As the glaciers get smaller, there is less ice to cool the air and less water for people to use. In some places, less water means more drought. In other places, however, melting glaciers causes more flooding.

The glaciers on the Himalayas are some of the fastest melting glaciers. The rapid melting of these glaciers may cause the major rivers below the mountains to flood the land around them.

What can we do?

Here are some ways we can help stop climate change. We can reduce our **carbon footprint**. A carbon footprint is how much carbon dioxide a person creates by using electricity, gasoline, and oil. How many of the things shown here will you do?

- In winter, open your curtains and let the sun help heat your home. Turn down the heat and wear a sweater if you feel cold.
- In summer, close the curtains to stop heat from coming in.
- To save water, take quick showers and turn off the water while brushing your teeth.
- Turn lights off when you are not in a room to save electricity.
- Turn off your computer when you are not using it.
- Wash your clothes in cold water instead of hot. Hang them outside to dry instead of using the dryer.

Try to walk lightly on Earth. What can you do to leave a smaller footprint?

Recycle paper, plastic, and aluminum. Put food scraps into a **compost** bin. Trade books and toys with your friends.

Plant trees in your yard or community. Trees remove carbon dioxide from the air.

Start a vegetable garden or buy food that was grown close to home. Trucks that bring food from far away use a lot of gasoline and oil and add to your footprint.

When possible, ride your bike instead of asking your parents to drive you in the car. A bike does not pollute the air because it uses no gasoline or oil.

Glossary

Note: Some boldfaced words are defined where they appear in the book.

breed To create offspring, or babies

condense To concentrate water droplets from gas into liquid form

compost Organic matter, such as plants, that decay

continent One of Earth's seven huge areas of land

current A flow of water in an ocean that moves continuously in a certain direction

drought A long period without rain

equator An imaginary line around the center of Earth where it is hot all year

evaporate To change a liquid, such as water, into a vapor, or mist

glacier A large, slow-moving body of ice

greenhouse gases Gases such as carbon dioxide that trap heat within the Earth's atmosphere

humid Describing air with a lot of water vapor in it

mist A cloud of tiny water droplets near the Earth's surface

permafrost A layer of permanently frozen soil that is beneath the top layer of soil

precipitation Any form of water, such as rain or snow, that falls to Earth's surface

temperate Describing a region of mild climate

temperature A measure of how hot or cold something is

Tropic of Cancer The northern boundary of the tropical zone

Tropic of Capricorn The southern boundary of the tropical zone

water vapor Tiny droplets of water

weather forecast A report explaining what the weather will be like on a particular day

Index